English Olympiad

Book 2

www.pegasusforkids.com

© **B. Jain Publishers (P) Ltd.** All rights reserved. No part of this book may be reproduced, stored in a retrieval system or transmitted, in any form or by any means, mechanical, photocopying, recording or otherwise, without any prior written permission of the publisher.

Published by Kuldeep Jain for B. Jain Publishers (P) Ltd., D-157, Sector 63, Noida - 201307, U.P.

Registered office: 1921/10, Chuna Mandi, Paharganj, New Delhi-110055

Printed in India at Narain Printers & Binder, Noida

Preface

English Olympiad Book–2 has been carefully written, designed and brought to fruition keeping in mind the requirements of the students. It has almost all necessary elements that make each exercise a learning experience for the children, their teachers and parents. It also ensures gradual progression from English Olympiad Book-1.

'Learning by doing' – the ethos behind introducing Olympiads is an effort to achieve perfection. In this spirit, we have followed a systematic pattern, inclusive of the scientific method and child-centric approach, wherein each concept has been explained again (as understood that it was done as part of grammar lessons). Therefore, revisions here leave enough room to substantiate upon experiential learning that help students to deliver better.

In the end of the book, we have also provided three test papers that carry a diverse set of questions. They will help children test themselves amidst all concepts put together in random order, which will bring greater degree of clarity and thought.

Salient Features

- Multiple choice questions
- Use of necessary illustrations to make learning simpler
- Model test papers in the end to make a wholesome assessment
- Inclusion of almost all aspects of English Olympiad exams

We wish all readers of **English Olympiad Book–2** a joyful experience.

CONTENTS

1. Jumbled Words and Sentences 5
2. Identify Objects and Monuments 10
3. Identify Animals and Young Ones 13
4. Identify Personalities and Professions 16
5. Synonyms 19
6. Antonyms 22
7. Nouns 25
8. Pronouns 28
9. Verbs 32
10. Adjectives 35
11. Prepositions 38
12. Articles 41
13. Singular and Plural 44
14. Analogy 46
15. Comprehension 49
    Model Test Paper-1 53
    Model Test Paper-2 56
    Model Test Paper-3 61

Answer Key 65

Jumbled Words and Sentences

Jumbled Words

Look at this word: THERFEA

Isn't it meaningless?

Let us rearrange the letters to make it meaningful: **FEATHER**

Here, **THERFEA** is a jumbled word. When the letters of a word are not in correct order, it is called a jumbled word.

We must rearrange jumbled words to make them meaningful.

EXERCISE 1

Rearrange the following words to make them meaningful.

1. **REATSE**
   a) ERATSE   b) EASTER
   c) ASTERE   d) TEREAS

2. **LUMNCO**
   a) NUMCOL   b) MULCON
   c) COLUMN   d) none of these

3. **TIONEDUCA**
   a) EDUCATION   b) CATIONEDU
   c) NEDUCATION   d) all of these

4. PATERNGNI

    a) INGPARENT   b) INGPTRENA

    c) PARENTING   d) all of these

5. EXCELTLEN

    a) TLENEXCELL   b) ENTLEXCEL

    c) EXCELTENL   d) EXCELLENT

6. SEVLEA

    a) LEAVES   b) EAVESL

    c) VESLEA   d) none of these

7. SUPREP

    a) SUPER   b) PURSER

    c) USURP   d) none of these

8. RYKEBA

    a) BAKERY   b) KERYBA

    c) BAKER   d) BAYRKE

9. NACHSPI

    a) PATRRO   b) PARROT

    c) PRROTA   d) SPINACH

10. ECSCIEN

    a) ECSCINE   b) SCIENCE

    c) ENSW   d) NEWS

Jumbled Sentences

Just as jumbled words, when the words of a sentence are not in order to make complete sense, then such a sentence is a called jumbled sentence.

For example:

Bakes cakes Tina.

This does not make any sense. Let us now rearrange the words to make a meaningful sentence:

Tina bakes cakes.

EXERCISE 2

Now rearrange these words to make a meaningful sentence.

1. **Suparna tailoring likes and needlework.**
   a) Tailoring needlework Suparna likes and.
   b) Suparna likes tailoring and needlework.
   c) Tailoring and needlework Suparna likes.
   d) None of these

2. **We can a happy India make together country.**
   a) Happy country together we can make a India.
   b) Together we can make India a happy country.
   c) Together we can make a happy country India.
   d) None of these

3. **Rich in minerals is India.**

    a) India is rich in minerals.

    b) Rich is India in minerals.

    c) India minerals is rich in.

    d) None of these

4. **Brazil is the producer largest of coffee in the world.**

    a) Largest producer is the Brazil of coffee in the world.

    b) Coffee is the largest producer of Brazil in the world.

    c) Brazil is the largest producer of coffee in the world.

    d) All of these

5. **I have breakfast and milk for eggs.**

    a) I have breakfast for milk and eggs.

    b) Milk and eggs for breakfast I have.

    c) I have milk for breakfast and eggs.

    d) None of these

6. **I enjoy storybooks reading.**

    a) I storybooks enjoy reading.

    b) Enjoy I storybooks reading.

    c) I enjoy reading storybooks.

    d) None of these

7. Must respect elders our we.
   a) Respect our elders we must.
   b) Our respect elders we must.
   c) Our elders we must respect.
   d) We must respect our elders.

8. National Bravery Awards Republic Day eve the are presented on.
   a) Eve presented are National Bravery Awards on the Republic Day.
   b) National Bravery Awards are presented on the Republic Day eve.
   c) On the Day Republic eve presented are National Bravery Awards.
   d) none of these.

9. Plants give us oxygen and trees.
   a) Trees give us oxygen and plants.
   b) Oxygen give us trees and plants.
   c) Give us oxygen, trees and plants.
   d) none of these.

10. Gandhi Mahatma is a memorial to Raj Ghat.
   a) Memorial to Raj Ghat is a Mahatma Gandhi.
   b) Mahatma Gandhi to Raj a Ghat is memorial.
   c) Memorial is Raj Ghat to a Mahatma Gandhi.
   d) Raj Ghat is a memorial to Mahatma Gandhi.

Identify Objects and Monuments

2

EXERCISE 1

Objects

Identify the pictures and tick (✓) the correct answers.

1. a) book b) cotton bud
   c) hammer d) napkin

2. a) ribbon b) doormat
   c) bubble d) balloon

3. a) feather b) wings of a plane
   c) token d) cat

4. a) tennis ball b) basketball
   c) cricket ball d) table tennis ball

5. a) aeroplane b) gas balloon
   c) space rocket d) helicopter

6. a) table b) chair
   c) sofa d) bed

7. a) hair oil b) comb
    c) hair dryer d) toothbrush

8. a) keys b) hammer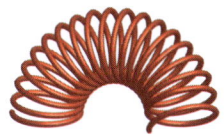
    c) spring d) lock

9. a) pipe b) water gun
    c) cup d) bucket

10. a) door b) window
    c) gate d) gateway

EXERCISE 2

Monuments

Identify the pictures and tick (✓) the correct answers.

1. a) Leaning Tower of Pisa b) Qutab Minar
    c) Eiffel Tower d) TV Tower

2. a) Taj Mahal b) Jal Mahal
    c) Rang Mahal d) Sheesh Mahal

3. a) Statue of Liberty b) Christ, the Redeemer
    c) Statue of Buddha d) Great Sphinx of Giza

4. a) Golden Temple   b) St. Peter's Basilica

    c) The Western Wall   d) Mahabodhi Temple

5. a) Humayun's Tomb   b) Pyramids of Giza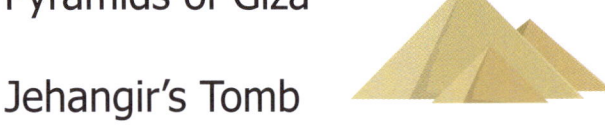

    c) Blue Domed Church   d) Jehangir's Tomb

6. a) Great Wall of China   b) Red Fort

    c) Purana Qila   d) City Palace

7. a) Gateway of India   b) India Gate

    c) Char Minar   d) Delhi Gate

8. a) Rashtrapati Bhawan   b) The White House

    c) Buckingham Palace   d) The Kremlin

9. a) Stonehenge   b) Mount Rushmore

    c) Capitol Hill   d) Sun Temple, Konark

10. a) Big Ben, London   b) Leaning Tower of Pisa

    c) Burj Khalifa   d) Empire State Building

Identify Animals and Young Ones

3

EXERCISE 1

Animals

Identify the pictures and tick (✓) the correct answers.

1. a) cow   b) tiger

   c) lion   d) snake

2. a) hyena   b) rhino

   c) yak   d) rat

3. a) frog   b) horse

   c) buffalo   d) cat

4. a) donkey   b) cat

   c) horse   d) mare

5. a) rabbit   b) dog

   c) bear   d) crocodile

6. a) alligator   b) lizard

   c) snake   d) leech

7. a) yak   b) rhino
    c) toad   d) mare

8. a) jaguar   b) leopard
    c) tiger   d) lion

9. a) zebra   b) rhino
    c) jaguar   d) deer

10. a) hippo   b) camel
    c) zebra   d) giraffe

EXERCISE 2

Young Ones

Identify the pictures and tick (✓) the correct answers.

1. a) foal   b) cub
    c) kitten   d) puppy

2. a) baby   b) duckling
    c) piglet   d) chick

3. a) joey   b) kitten
    c) lamb   d) calf

4. a) calf b) duckling

   c) chick d) fawn

5. a) kitten b) lamb

   c) calf d) cub

6. a) puppy b) kitten

   c) piglet d) fawn

7. a) cub b) kitten

   c) piglet d) lamb

8. a) lamb b) chick

   c) fawn d) cub

9. a) puppy b) kitten

   c) chick d) joey

10. a) cub b) lamb

    c) foal d) piglet

Identify Personalities and Professions

EXERCISE 1

Personalities

Identify the pictures and tick (✓) the correct answers.

1. a) Mahatma Gandhi   b) Martin Luther King, Jr.
   c) Barack Obama   d) Nelson Mandela

2. a) Sachin Tendulkar b) Kapil Dev
   c) Sania Mirza   d) Saina Nehwal

3. a) Shahrukh Khan   b) Amitabh Bachchan
   c) Kareena Kapoor   d) Karan Johar

4. a) Martin Luther King b) Barack Obama
   c) Narendra Modi   d) Manmohan Singh

5. a) Narendra Modi   b) APJ Abdul Kalam
   c) Raghuram Rajan   d) Akshay Kumar

6. a) Mahatma Gandhi   b) Martin Luther King
   c) Narendra Modi   d) Nelson Mandela

7.   a) APJ Abdul Kalam   b) Sonia Gandhi

      c) Rahul Gandhi   d) Pratibha Patil

8.   a) Deepika Padukone   b) Priyanka Chopra

      c) Indira Gandhi   d) Katrina Kaif

9.   a) Kiran Bedi   b) Saina Nehwal

      c) Sarojini Naidu   d) Nafisa Ali

10.   a) Mahatma Gandhi   b) Martin Luther King

      d) Nelson Mandela   d) None of these

Professions

Identify the pictures and tick (✓) the correct answers.

1.   a) carpenter   b) doctor

      c) policeman   d) scientist

2.   a) doctor   b) blacksmith

      c) goldsmith   d) None of these

3.   a) architect   b) scientist

      c) curator   d) doctor

4. a) painter   b) driver

    c) tailor   d) actress

5. a) curator   b) blacksmith

    c) driver   d) tailor

6. a) postman   b) doctor

    c) scientist   d) None of these

7. a) salesman   b) policeman

    c) painter   d) scientist

8. a) curator   b) watchman

    c) driver   d) sculptor

9. a) soldier   b) pilot

    c) sailor   d) salesman

10. a) shopkeeper   b) farmer

     c) sculptor   d) architect

SYNONYMS

A word that means exactly or nearly the same as another word is called a **synonym**.

For example:
Close is a synonym of **Shut**.

EXERCISE 1

Tick (✓) the synonyms of these words:

1. **Abandon**
   a) Ample   b) Worship
   c) Leave   d) Idolize

2. **Alive**
   a) Lively   b) Improve
   c) Happy   d) Sad

3. **Brave**
   a) Fearless   b) Move
   c) Terror   d) Frighten

4. **Pause**
   a) Move   b) Slow
   c) Quiet   d) Stop

5. **Big**

a) Decide b) Body

c) Huge d) Head

6. **Disease**

a) Happy b) Direct

c) Health d) Sickness

7. **Keen**

a) Meet b) Eager

c) Learn d) Assistant

8. **Happy**

a) Glad b) Deliver

c) Guide d) Brain

9. **Enemy**

a) Partner b) Fellow

c) Foe d) Friend

10. **Hug**

a) Embrace b) Tight

c) Help d) Play

EXERCISE 2

Mina is writing an essay. Help her with synonyms of some words so that she can avoid repeating those words in sentences.

Choose from the options given below and write against the correct words.

| Feeling | Open | Need | Sufficient | Real |
| Needy | Clear | Gloomy | Total | Achieve |

1. Bright _____

2. Dull _____

3. Earn _____

4. Frank _____

5. Emotion _____

6. Enough _____

7. Poor _____

8. Want _____

9. Whole _____

10. Pure _____

ANTONYMS

Look at the words given below.

Poor - Rich

Such words which are completely opposite in meaning are called **antonyms**.

EXERCISE 1

Match the following words with their antonyms.

1. Polite   Open

2. Negative   South

3. Victory   Rude

4. Smile   Awake

5. Shut   Safety

6. Future   Past

7. Asleep   Defeat

8. Inhale   Exhale

9. Danger   Positive

10. North   Frown

EXERCISE 2

Tick (✓) the antonyms of these words.

1. **Singular**
   a) Enough					b) Leave
   c) Ample					d) Plural

2. **Dead**
   a) Sad					b) Improve
   c) Alive					d) Happy

3. **Coward**
   a) Brave					b) Hope
   c) Scared					d) Fearful

4. **Common**
   a) Same					b) Quiet
   c) Rare					d) None of these

5. **Master**
   a) Big					b) Head
   c) Servant					d) Male

6. Before

a) Earlier

b) After

c) Yesterday

d) Past

7. Absent

a) Before

b) Past

c) Present

d) Earlier

8. Hit

a) Force

b) Strike

c) Deliver

d) Miss

9. Faithful

a) Unfaithful

b) Lucky

c) Great

d) Happy

10. Proud

a) Playful

b) Humble

c) Old

d) Silence

Nouns

Nouns are naming words for persons, places or things.

For example:
Kailash, Mumbai, Australia, Television, Duck, etc.

There are various kinds of nouns.

Proper Nouns: Names of particular persons, places or things that necessarily start with a capital letter are called **proper nouns**.

For example:
Rahul, New Delhi, Pluto, etc.

Common Nouns: General names of persons, places or things are called **common nouns**.

For example:
girl, city, planet, etc.

Countable Nouns: Nouns that can be physically counted are called **countable nouns**.

For example:
car, house, cart, etc.

EXERCISE 1

Uncountable Nouns: Nouns that cannot be physically counted and cannot be denoted by a number are called **uncountable nouns**. In the singular form, such words are prefixed with a or an.

For example:
happiness, cruelty, wood, etc.

Which of these words are nouns? Tick (✓) the correct answers.

1. a) open b) close c) diary d) good

2. a) hangar b) landing c) moving d) inside

Which of these words are proper nouns? Tick (✓) the correct answers.

3. a) boot b) shoe c) Reebok d) shelf

4. a) Statue of Liberty b) New York c) United States of America d) All of these

Which of these are common nouns? Tick (✓) the correct answers.

5. a) Air India b) plane c) take-off d) France

6. a) departed b) Shatabdi Express c) train d) faster

Which of these are countable nouns. Tick (✓) the correct answers.

7. a) sons b) crowd c) milk d) water

8. a) children   b) cubs
    c) ducklings   d) All the above

Which of these are uncountable nouns. Tick (✓) the correct answers.

9. a) chairs   b) steel
    c) glasses   d) plates

10. a) trucks   b) lorries
    c) traffic   d) buses

EXERCISE 2

Underline the correct options in the following.

1. BBC   (Proper Noun/Common Noun)
2. Game   (Uncountable Noun/Common Noun)
3. Water   (Uncountable Noun/Proper Noun)
4. Books   (Proper Noun/Countable Noun)
5. Amazon River   (Common Noun/Proper Noun)
6. Mountains   (Common Noun/Proper Noun)
7. Security   (Proper Noun/Uncountable Noun)
8. Swimming Pool   (Proper Noun/Common Noun)
9. Dennis   (Proper Noun/Countable Noun)
10. Parents   (Proper Noun/Common Noun)

PRONOUNS

Pronouns are words that can be used in place of nouns.

For example:

John is reading a book. **John** enjoys reading.

John, here is repetitive. To avoid that, we could rewrite the above sentences as:

John is reading a book. **He** enjoys reading.

Here, we have used **He** in place of **John**, which is a **noun**. Therefore, **He** is a **pronoun**.

I, she, he, you, we, they, it are **pronouns**.

EXERCISE 1

Tick (✓) the correct options.

1. **Which of these are pronouns?**
   a) they
   b) it
   c) she
   d) all of these

2. **Which of the following nouns could be replaced by the pronoun 'it'?**
   a) India Gate
   b) Sahiba
   c) Soldiers
   d) Parents

3. **Which of these deserves a pronoun?**
    a) for b) children

    c) as d) is

4. **Cinderella and Snow White – which pronoun can replace these names?**
    a) it b) she

    c) he d) none

5. **He just bought a machine. Let us see if _____ works.**
    a) they b) it

    c) she d) it's

6. **Who is that boy walking in the corridor? Bring _____ to me, now.**
    a) he or she b) it or they

    c) him d) you

7. **Which of these can be replaced by a pronoun?**
    a) flying b) hosting

    c) flag d) hoisting

8. **Which of these cannot be replaced by a pronoun?**
    a) lamp b) chair

    c) sit d) table

9. **We must be together at all times. Which word in this sentence is a pronoun?**

a) times　　　　　　　　　　　　b) together

c) must　　　　　　　　　　　　d) We

10. Did you know that a whale is a mammal? Which word in this sentence can be replaced by a pronoun?

a) mammal　　　　　　　　　　b) whale

c) know　　　　　　　　　　　d) whale and mammal

EXERCISE 2

Tick (✓) the correct pronouns for the underlined or missing words.

1. That child is homeless.
a) He or She　　　　　　　　　b) She

c) He　　　　　　　　　　　　d) It

2. Where are _____ going to have breakfast?
a) she　　　　　　　　　　　　b) he

c) it　　　　　　　　　　　　 d) they

3. Dr Sharma understands his patients well.
a) he or she　　　　　　　　　b) he

c) doctor　　　　　　　　　　 d) they

4. The boys are playing well. _____ may bring the trophy home.
a) It　　　　　　　　　　　　 b) He

c) They　　　　　　　　　　　d) None of these

5. _____ is important to work hard.
   a) He   b) It
   c) She   d) It's

6. **The scientists are launching the satellite today. _____ will fetch us information about the weather.**
   a) He or She   b) It or They
   c) It   d) Him

7. **Most birds fly.**
   a) They   b) She and Her
   c) She and Him   d) He and She

8. **Mammals give birth to their young ones.**
   a) They   b) He
   c) She   d) The boys

9. **Mahatma Gandhi is known as the father of our nation.**
   a) Her and She   b) Girl and Boy
   c) He   d) She and He

10. **My name is Varun. _____ am six years old.**
    a) I   b) They
    c) She   d) He

Verbs

A word that depicts an action is called a **verb**.

For example:

Run, **Play**, **Jump**, etc.

Let us use these in sentences to understand them better.
She **runs** very fast.
They **play** well.
I can **jump** across the wall.

Here, words **runs**, **play** and **jump** show actions. Therefore, they are verbs.

EXERCISE 1

Which of these are verbs? Tick (✓) the correct options.

1. a) call   b) telephone
   c) loud   d) None of these

2. a) chair   b) sofa
   c) table   d) sit

3. a) sing   b) beautiful
   c) nice   d) good

4. a) date   b) mark
   c) day   d) calendar

5. a) fish b) shoal
   c) swim d) none of these

6. a) soldier b) brave
   c) enemy d) none of these

7. a) ground b) football
   c) play d) well

8. a) cheerful b) cheer
   c) team d) good

9. a) banana b) apple
   c) eat d) fruit

10. a) you b) yours
    c) keep d) safely

EXERCISE 2

Choose the correct verbs from the brackets and fill in the blanks.

1. Dolphins _____ in seas and oceans. (fly/live/rely)

2. The guests are _____ for dinner. (swimming/coming/sleeping)

3. They are going to _____ their anniversary. (jump/call/celebrate)

4. Good people _____ the world a better place. (make/bake/play)

5. Horses _____ on the fields. (close/gallop/jump)

6. The watchman _____ our homes at night. (walks/crawls/guards)

7. The referee will _____ the whistle. (blow/sweep/hunt)

8. The hunter _____ the lion. (bleat/ran/shot)

9. Let us _____ what to do next. (think/call/jump)

10. The pirates _____ the seamen. (frightened/rolled/crawled)

ADJECTIVES

Words such as **lovely**, **happy** or **sad** tell us something about a noun. Such words are called **adjectives**.

EXERCISE 1

Which of these are adjectives?

1. a) clean   b) car
   c) window   d) tool

2. a) bracket   b) sign
   c) easy   d) distance

3. a) caller   b) soft-spoken
   c) telephone   d) booth

4. a) task   b) energetic
   c) energy   d) finish

5. a) flowers   b) rose
   c) smell   d) beautiful

6. a) gold   b) shining
   c) sell   d) buy

7. a) amazing	b) magician

    c) trick	d) today

8. a) hit	b) face

    c) belt	d) hard

9. a) bullet	b) trains

    c) supersonic	d) speed

10. a) Gulmarg	b) scenic

    c) Kashmir	d) mountains

EXERCISE 2

Fill in the blanks with the correct adjectives.

1. **The police officer is an _____ man.**
   a) girl	b) person

   c) honest	d) none of these

2. **Jasmine is as _____ as a schoolgirl.**
   a) lady	b) person

   c) bashful	d) none of these

3. **The Burj Khalifa in Dubai is the _____ building in the world.**
   a) tallest	b) good

   c) huge	d) hotel

4. **The bee hummingbird is the _____ bird in the world.**
a) bird					b) smallest

c) animal					d) feather

5. **The blue whale is the _____ animal of all times.**
a) fish					b) mammal

c) shark					d) largest

6. **Simone is reading an _____ book.**
a) interesting				b) yellow

c) square					d) white

7. **The mechanic fixed the _____ car.**
a) broken					b) high

c) bridge					d) none of these

8. **Mr Smith's _____ son is finishing college.**
a) daughter				b) eldest

c) children				d) none of these

9. **How do my _____ glasses look?**
a) yours					b) quick

c) his					d) new

10. **We stayed beneath a _____ tree.**
a) interesting				b) shady

c) like					d) none

PREPOSITIONS

A word that expresses relation between a noun or pronoun and another word is called a **preposition**.

For example:

She went **into** the room.

In this sentence **into** shows relationship between verb (went) and noun (room). So it is a **preposition**.

EXERCISE 1

Tick (✓) the correct prepositions and fill in the blanks.

1. What is the celebration _____?
    a) to
    b) for
    c) of
    d) at

2. The maneater is _____ the jungle.
    a) on
    b) under
    c) in
    d) between

3. The Jungle Book was written _____ Rudyard Kipling.
    a) in
    b) by
    c) over
    d) of

4. He works _____ his boss.

a) at

b) behind

c) under

d) by

5. He ordered a burger _____ the soft drink.

a) for

b) behind

c) between

d) with

6. She is allergic _____ dust.

a) on

b) at

c) to

d) over

7. Ramit was born _____ 2007.

a) in

b) below

c) under

d) over

8. I am looking _____ my keys.

a) for

b) in

c) with

d) to

9. He hasn't smoked _____ ages.

a) with

b) between

c) for

d) to

10. **The plane flew _____ our house.**
   a) at b) over
   c) between d) under

EXERCISE 2

Choose the correct options to fill in the blanks.

1. You can look up the word _____ a dictionary. (on/in/none)

2. Who were you thinking _____ ? (on/of/behind)

3. The robber was standing _____ Mr Jones when he stabbed him. (behind/at/across)

4. The secretariat is _____ the airport. (over/between/near)

5. The President was standing _____ the Prime Minister. (with/between/across)

6. India lies _____ Bangladesh and Pakistan. (between/across/in front of)

7. Birds can fly _____ seas and oceans. (across/under/below)

8. India's national anthem was written _____ Rabindranath Tagore. (over/by/with)

9. We must pay attention _____ our teachers. (to/with/across)

10. She will perform _____ the audience? (in front of/in/on)

ARTICLES

A, **an** and **the** are called articles. They are used before a noun or an adjective.

For example:

a building, **an** apple, **the** President of America

EXERCISE 1

Fill in the blanks with the correct articles- a, an or the whichever is correct.

1. _____ Nehru Planetarium will be closed today.

2. It is _____ class activity.

3. India is _____ vast nation.

4. _____ Taj Mahal is _____ wonder of _____ the world.

5. Punjab means _____ land of five rivers.

6. I read _____ interesting book yesterday.

7. I wish to become _____ doctor.

8. Who is jumping from _____ window?

9. May I make _____ phone call?

10. _____ internet has not been working.

EXERCISE 2

Tick (✓) the correct options.

1. **Kolkata is _____ capital of West Bengal.**
   a) a   b) an
   c) the   d) none of these

2. **We had _____ good time last evening.**
   a) a   b) an
   c) the   d) none of these

3. **We were scared of _____ snakes.**
   a) a   b) an
   c) the   d) none of thesee

4. **In which museum are _____ swords kept?**
   a) a   b) an
   c) the   d) none of these

5. **He had _____ injury during the match.**
   a) a   b) an
   c) the   d) none of these

6. **It was _____ amazing debate.**
   a) a   b) an
   c) the   d) none of these

7. _____ time has come when we should make India clean.

a) A b) An

c) The d) None of these

8. He is _____ handsome officer.

a) a b) an

c) the d) none of these

9. _____ painting is yet to be seen.

a) A b) An

c) The d) None of these

10. We had _____ grand feast on his birthday.

a) a b) an

c) the d) none of these

Singular and Plural

A single noun (**bottle** or **bench**) counted as one is called **singular**. When there is more than one noun (**bottles** or **benches**), we call them **plural**.

EXERCISE 1

Write if the words given below are singular or plural.

1. cows _____
2. birds _____
3. leaf _____
4. pen _____
5. notebook _____
6. stories _____
7. tyres _____
8. plate _____
9. animal _____
10. river _____

EXERCISE 2

Tick (✓) the correct plural forms of the words given below.

1. **house**
   a) houses   b) houss

2. **hour**
   a) houres   b) hours

3. **exercise**
   a) exercises   b) exerciss

4. **speaker**
   a) speakerss   b) speakers

5. **cabbage**
   a) cabbages   b) cabbags

6. **village**
   a) villagees   b) villages

7. **lady**
   a) ladys   b) ladies

8. **mountain**
   a) mountains   b) mountaines

9. **calendar**
   a) calendares   b) calendars

10. **gardener**
    a) gardeneres   b) gardeners

ANALOGY

14

An **analogy** is a comparison between one thing and another in order to explain a similarity in purpose or of a situation.

For example:

If pilot is to airplane then driver is to car. You may also write it as:

pilot : airplane :: driver : car

Fill in the blanks with the correct words.

1. If left is to right then up is to _____. (down/after)

2. If ear is to _____ then nose is to smell. (touch/hear)

3. If _____ is to hot then winter is to cold. (summer/rains)

4. If _____ is to winter then T-shirt is to summer. (coat/raincoat)

5. If India is to Indians then _____ is to Japanese. (Japan/Korea)

6. If tiger is to den then dog is to _____. (kennel/jungle)

7. If school is to teacher then hospital is to _____. (nurse/soldier)

8. If leaf is to tree then bristle is to _____. (brush/ground)

9. If knife is to cut then _____ is to write. (book/pencil)

10. If dinner is to night then lunch is to _____. (afternoon/morning)

46

EXERCISE 2

Tick (✓) the correct option.

1. **green : grass :: _____ : sky**
   a) white
   b) pink
   c) orange
   d) blue

2. **letter : paper :: painting : _____**
   a) canvas
   b) paper
   c) leaf
   d) wood

3. **lights : Diwali :: tinsels : _____**
   a) Id
   b) Christmas
   c) Gurpurab
   d) Janamashtmi

4. **Gandhi Jayanti : Mahatma Gandhi :: Children's Day : _____**
   a) Jawaharlal Nehru
   b) Subhash Chandra Bose
   c) Bhagat Singh
   d) Sarojini Naidu

5. **eat : hungry :: sleep : _____**
   a) happy
   b) tired
   c) alert
   d) none of these

6. **dead : _____ :: wet : dry**
   a) sleep
   b) tired
   c) good
   d) alive

7. **silence : quiet :: loud : _____**
   a) happy
   b) sensible
   c) noisy
   d) wonderful

8. **desk : classroom :: _____ : theatre**
   a) table
   b) almirah
   c) screen
   d) pen

9. **soap : wash :: _____ : buy**
   a) money
   b) powder
   c) apple
   d) phone

10. **apron : kitchen :: uniform : _____**
    a) holiday
    b) picnic
    c) school
    d) movie

COMPREHENSION

EXERCISE 1

Read the passage given above and fill in the blanks with the correct options.

The Ant and the Grasshopper

On a summer's day, a Grasshopper was singing, chirping and hopping around in a field. He saw an Ant carrying some corn to his nest.

"Come, let's chat for a bit," said the Grasshopper. "I am sorry, I can't. I am collecting some food for the winter," said the Ant. "Why bother about winter?" said the Grasshopper, "It's four months away."

But the Ant was determined. It kept collecting food. When the winter came, the Grasshopper had no food. It could only see the Ant feeding itself with comfort.

1. The _____ was singing, chirping and hopping around?
   (Ant/Grasshopper)

2. The Ant was carrying some _____ to his nest.
   (corn/grass)

3. The _____ asked the _____ to chat with him.
   (Ant/Grasshopper)

4. The _____ was collecting food for the winter.
   (Ant/Grasshopper)

5. When the winter came, the _____ had nothing to eat.
   (Ant/Grasshopper)

EXERCISE 2

Poem

Little Things

Little drops of water,
Little grains of sand,
Make the mighty ocean
And the beauteous land.

Little deeds of kindness,
Little words of love,
Make our earth an Eden,
Like the heaven above.

-Julia A. Carney

Read the poem given above and tick (✓) the correct options.

1. **What makes the ocean mighty?**
   a) little drops of water
   b) little grains of sand
   c) rain
   d) storm

2. **What makes the land beautiful?**
   a) little drops of water
   b) little grains of sand
   c) rain
   d) storm

3. **What makes the Earth like heaven?**
   a) love and kindness
   b) Eden
   c) sand
   d) water

4. **What do you think Eden could mean?**

   a) bitter b) garden of hate

   c) sour d) garden of love

5. **Overall, is the poet telling us about little things that destroy the Earth?**

   a) Yes b) No

EXERCISE 3

Speaking and Writing

Choose the correct answers.

1. **Do you say "Hi" to the people you don't know?**

   a) Yes b) No

2. **Which of these would sound polite over the telephone?**

   a) Who are you?

   b) You need to call later.

   c) Could I please take down a message?

   d) None of these

Now choose a reply for the following:

3. **May I speak to your father, please?**

   a) Of course, not.

   b) Yes, you can.

c) Take it.

d) Sure, please hold on.

4. **Thank you for your hospitality.**

   a) It's fine.

   b) You are welcome.

   c) Never mind.

   d) Ok.

5. **Which of these can be termed as a rude behaviour?**

   a) See you, soon!

   b) We must meet again.

   c) Don't waste my time.

   d) Thank you, it was a good day.

Model Test Paper-I

Choose the correct words from the brackets and fill in the blanks.

1. Who is _____ the door? (on/at/with)

2. Can _____ host a party tomorrow? (her/him/we)

3. book : library :: aeroplane : _____ (hangar/drawer/garage)

4. NOCTTO is a jumbled word for _____ (TOKEN/COTTON)

5. _____ Pacific Ocean is _____ largest ocean in _____ world. (an/the/it)

6. Plural of leaf is _____ (leaves/leafs)

7. Who is _____ strongest out of all? (a/an/the)

8. She was _____ hurt in the game. (badly/nicely/happily)

9. You must understand _____ problem. (her/him/she)

10. He is _____ officer in the Navy. (a/an/the)

Write singular or plural.

11. tower _____ (singular/plural)

12. gates _____ (singular/plural)

13. pipe _____ (singular/plural)

14. cigarette _____ (singular/plural)

15. glass _____ (singular/plural)

Identify the correct pictures.

16. a) sweets b) cakes
    c) toffees d) muffins

17. a) yak b) rhinoceros
    c) goat d) hippopotamus

18. a) jewellery b) clothes
    c) shoes d) caps

19. a) erasers b) pens
    c) pencils d) stationery box

20. a) India Gate b) Gateway of India
    c) Charminar d) Red Fort

Choose the correct options and fill in the blanks.

21. 'A', 'an' and 'the' are called _____.
    (articles/prepositions/adjectives)

22. Which _____ will fight his case? (doctor/lawyer/policeman)

23. The _____ hangs criminals to death.
    (policeman/hangman/soldier)

24. Mud is a _____ noun. (countable/uncountable)

25. The word 'delicious' is an _____. (noun/adjective/preposition)

26. The synonym of gloomy is _____. (dull/happy/glad)

27. 'Cure' is a _____. (verb/adjective)

28. 'Happy' and 'sad' are _____. (prepositions/antonyms/synonyms)

29. If day is to light, then night is to _____.
(bright/glowing/dark)

30. What word can you make by rearranging the jumbled letters 'terucomp'? _____ (compteru/computer/uterpomc)

Model Test Paper-2

Tick (✓) the correct names of the given pictures.

1. a) metro rail   b) engine

   c) trolley   d) bus

2. a) plane   b) helicopter

   c) racing car   d) motorbike

3. a) nail   b) toe

   c) finger   d) knee

4. a) bread   b) butter

   c) jam   d) honey

5. a) burger   b) sandwich

   c) pizza   d) chips

Are these singular or plural?

6. toe _____ (singular/plural)

7. bells _____ (singular/plural)

8. wagon _____ (singular/plural)

9. batteries _____ (singular/plural)

10. hammer _____ (singular/plural)

Read the passage given below and answer the questions that follow:

Samarth was the captain of his school basketball team. He was very keen to make a good team for the school. He believed in giving everybody a chance.

Rahul was a disabled boy who could not use his left hand. He was always on the wheelchair. He loved to play basketball. When he came to Samarth, other boys laughed at him. But, Samarth wanted to give him a chance.

Rahul was trained so well that he scored the highest in the inter-school tournament. Rahul and Samarth together showed the trophy to all those boys who laughed at Rahul. In this way, Samarth showed true spirit of a sportsman.

11. Who was Samarth?

   a) He was captain of the school cricket team.
   b) He was captain of the school basketball team.
   c) He was a player in the hockey team.
   d) All of these.

12. What did he believe in?

   a) To give everyone a chance to play in the basketball team.
   b) To join the school dance troupe.
   c) To become a good debater.
   d) None of these.

13. Rahul...

    a) was a disabled boy.

    b) worked with his left hand.

    c) did not play any game.

    d) none of these

14. Which of these sentences is false?

    a) Other boys in the team laughed at Rahul.

    b) Rahul laughed at other boys after becoming the highest scorer.

    c) Rahul was trained to join the basketball team.

    d) All of these

15. This story speaks about

    a) A sportman's true spirit.

    b) Samarth and Rahul's friendship.

    c) Samarth wanting to teach a lesson to the other boys.

    d) All of these

Choose the correct options.

16. MHAMRE is the jumbled word for hammering. _____
    (true/false)

17. Mrs. Mehra teaches children in a school. She is a _____.
    (coach/teacher/counsellor)

18. Statue of Liberty is a _____.
    (proper noun/common noun/pronoun)

19. Night is the meaning of Day. _____ (true/false)

20. Parents _____ for their children. (care/teach/talk)

Which of these are not adjectives? Put a cross (X) against each answer.

21. a) happy   b) run

    c) sad   d) cool

22. a) zoo   b) lazy

    c) swift   d) windy

23. a) pizza   b) delicious

    c) spicy   d) sumptuous

24. a) three   b) four

    c) five   d) science

25. a) attractive   b) good

    c) better   d) actor

Which of these are not pronouns? Put a cross (X) against each answer.

26. a) Caren   b) He

    c) She   d) It

27. a) People   b) They

    c) Her   d) He

Which of these are not verbs? Put a cross (X) against each answer.

28. a) parent   b) care

     c) work   d) play

29. a) office   b) people

     c) workers   d) all of these

30. a) kick   b) sprint

     c) open   d) player

MODEL TEST PAPER-3

Tick (✓) the correct gender.

1. Lioness
   a) masculine
   b) feminine
   c) common
   d) none of these

2. Duchess
   a) masculine
   b) feminine
   c) common
   d) none of these

3. Scientist
   a) masculine
   b) feminine
   c) common
   d) none of these

4. Tigress
   a) masculine
   b) feminine
   c) common
   d) none of these

5. Woman
   a) masculine
   b) feminine
   c) common
   d) none of these

6. Secretary
   a) masculine
   b) feminine
   c) common
   d) none of these

7. Queen
   a) masculine   b) feminine
   c) common   d) none of these

8. Czar
   a) masculine   b) feminine
   c) common   d) none of these

9. Peacock
   a) masculine   b) feminine
   c) common   d) none of these

10. Iron
    a) masculine   b) feminine
    c) common   d) none of these

Tick (✓) the correct options.

11. Celina is getting _____ dress stitched.
    a) a   b) an
    c) the   d) none of these

12. The Tower of Pisa is _____ attractive monument.
    a) a   b) an
    c) the   d) none of these

13. Rajiv has bought _____ two cars.
    a) a   b) an

    c) the   d) none of these

14. Would you shut _____ door, please?
    a) a   b) an

    c) the   d) none of these

15. Mrs Mehta is _____ mother of two children.
    a) a   b) an

    c) the   d) none of these

Fill in the blanks with the correct option. The illustrations will help you.

16. The students are sitting _____ of their teacher. (behind/across/in front of)

17. The cat is lying _____ the table. (over/under/above)

18. The policeman is watching from _____ the road. (over/behind/across)

19. The tower is _____ the fire station. (near/far/across)

20. The boy is swimming _____ the pool. (near/in/on)

Write if the words given below are singular or plural.

21. Glasses _____ (singular/plural)

22. Pencils _____ (singular/plural)

23. Computer _____ (singular/plural)

24. Plants _____ (singular/plural)

25. Chair _____ (singular/plural)

Fill in the blanks with the correct words.

26. The opposite of lazy is _____. (lazy/hot/active)

27. 'Huge' is an _____ . (adjective/noun/verb)

28. 'A', 'an' and 'the' are _____. (prepositions/articles/nouns)

29. 'He', 'she' and 'it' are _____ . (articles/pronouns/nouns)

30. What word can you make by rearranging the jumbled letters 'unon'?
    _____

Answer Key

Chapter 1
Exercise 1

1. b	2. c	3. a	4. c
5. d	6. a	7. d	8. a
9. d	10. b		

Exercise 2

1. b	2. b	3. a	4. c
5. d	6. c	7. d	8. b
9. d	10. d		

Chapter 2
Exercise 1

1. a	2. c	3. a	4. b
5. c	6. c	7. b	8. c
9. c	10. b		

Exercise 2

1. b	2. a	3. a	4. b
5. b	6. a	7. b	8. c
9. d	10. a		

Chapter 3
Exercise 1

1. d	2. a	3. b	4. a
5. c	6. a	7. b	8. b
9. d	10. c		

Exercise 2

1. a	2. b	3. d	4. c
5. b	6. a	7. b	8. c
9. d	10. a		

Chapter 4
Exercise 1

1. c	2. c	3. a	4. a
5. c	6. c	7. a	8. b
9. a	10. a		

Exercise 2

1. b	2. c	3. b	4. c
5. b	6. a	7. b	8. b
9. c	10. b		

Chapter 5
Exercise 1

| 1. c | 2. a | 3. a | 4. d |

5. c	6. d	7. b	8. a
9. c	10. a		

Exercise 2

1. Clear	2. Gloomy	3. Achieve
4. Open	5. Feeling	6. Sufficient
7. Needy	8. Need	9. Total
10. Real		

Chapter 6

Exercise 1

1. Rude	2. Positive	3. Defeat
4. Frown	5. Open	6. Past
7. Awake	8. Exhale	9. Safety
10. South		

Exercise 2

1. d	2. c	3. a	4. c
5. c	6. b	7. c	8. d
9. a	10. b		

Chapter 7

Exercise 1

1. c	2. a	3. c	4. d
5. b	6. c	7. a	8. d
9. b	10. c		

Exercise 2

1. Proper Noun
2. Common Noun
3. Uncountable Noun
4. Countable Noun
5. Proper Noun
6. Common Noun
7. Uncountable Noun
8. Common Noun
9. Proper Noun
10. Common Noun

Chapter 8
Exercise 1

1. d	2. a	3. b	4. b
5. b	6. c	7. c	8. c
9. d	10. d		

Exercise 2

1. a	2. d	3. b	4. c
5. b	6. c	7. a	8. a
9. c	10. a		

Chapter 9
Exercise 1

1. a	2. d	3. a	4. b
5. c	6. d	7. c	8. b
9. c	10. c		

Exercise 2

1. live	2. coming	3. celebrate
4. make	5. gallop	6. guards
7. blow	8. shot	9. think
10. frightened		

Chapter 10
Exercise 1

1. a	2. c	3. b	4. b
5. d	6. b	7. a	8. d
9. c	10. b		

Exercise 2

1. c	2. c	3. a	4. b
5. d	6. a	7. a	8. b
9. d	10. b		

Chapter 11
Exercise 1

1. b	2. c	3. b	4. c
5. d	6. c	7. a	8. a
9. c	10. b		

Exercise 2

1. in	2. of	3. behind	4. near
5. with	6. between	7. across	8. by
9. to	10. in front of		

Chapter 12
Exercise 1

1. The	2. a	3. a	4. The, a, the
5. the	6. an	7. a	8. the
9. a	10. the		

Exercise 2

1. c	2. a	3. c	4. c
5. b	6. b	7. c	8. a
9. c	10. a		

Chapter 13
Exercise 1

1. plural	2. plural	3. singular
4. singular	5. singular	6. plural
7. plural	8. singular	9. singular
10. singular		

Exercise 2

1. a	2. b	3. a	4. b
5. a	6. b	7. b	8. a
9. b	10. b		

Chapter 14
Exercise 1

1. down
2. hear
3. summer
4. coat
5. Japan
6. kennel
7. nurse
8. brush
9. pencil
10. afternoon

Exercise 2

1. d
2. a
3. b
4. a
5. b
6. d
7. c
8. c
9. a
10. c

Chapter 15
Exercise 1

1. Grasshopper
2. corn
3. Grasshopper, Ant
4. Ant
5. Grasshopper

Exercise 2

1. a
2. b
3. a
4. d
5. b

Exercise 3

1. b
2. c
3. d
4. b
5. c

Model Test Paper-1

1. at 2. we 3. hangar 4. COTTON 5. the, the, the 6. leaves 7. the 8. badly 9. her 10. an 11. singular 12. plural 13. singular 14. singular 15. singular 16. d 17. c 18. a 19. d 20. d 21. articles 22. lawyer 23. hangman 24. uncountable 25. adjective 26. dull 27. verb 28. antonyms 29. dark 30. computer.

Model Test Paper-2

1. metro rail 2. helicopter 3. knee 4. honey 5. pizza 6. singular 7. plural 8. singular 9. plural 10. singular 11. b 12. a 13. a 14. b 15. a 16. false 17. teacher 18. proper noun 19. false 20. care 21. b 22. a 23. a 24. d 25. d 26. a 27. a 28. a 29. d 30. d.

Model Test Paper-3

1. b 2. b 3. c 4. b 5. b 6. c 7. b 8. a 9. a 10. d 11. a 12. b 13. d 14. c 15. a 16. in front of 17. under 18. across 19. near 20. in 21. plural 22. plural 23. singular 24. plural 25. singular 26. active 27. adjective 28. articles 29. pronouns 30. noun.